THE ILLUSION OF PROSPERITY AND FREEDOM IN A FAILING SYSTEM

CANADA'S MIRAGE

NEOBORN CAVEMAN

*To all those freedom-lovers
who still have functioning brain cells*

Table of Content

Prologue

Control systems don't announce themselves through proclamations or sudden changes. They emerge through seemingly reasonable responses to manufactured crises. Each solution appears necessary, each change justified, each erosion of freedom rational —until the architecture of control stands complete.

Canada's transformation from a land of opportunity to a testing ground for sophisticated control systems follows this proven pattern. Understanding this transformation requires seeing how separate crises—housing, healthcare, cost of living—advance a unified agenda of surveillance and control.

This isn't speculation about future possibilities. The evidence exists in legislation being passed, systems being implemented, and infrastructure being built today. The only question is whether Canadians will recognize these patterns before acceptance becomes mandatory.

Over the past three decades, Canada has undergone a profound transformation that few have fully grasped. What appears as a series of distinct crises - housing unaffordability, cost of living increases, healthcare strain, and immigration pressures - masks a deeper, more systematic reconstruction of Canadian society. This book exposes the hidden architecture of control being built through these manufactured crises.

The Canada of 1988 stands in stark contrast to today's reality. Then, a family with one average income could afford a home in most major cities. Public services functioned effectively. Privacy was a right, not a luxury. Today, even dual-income professionals struggle to rent in urban centres. Healthcare wait times stretch for months. Every transaction, movement, and interaction feeds expanding surveillance networks.

This transformation isn't happening by accident. Each crisis creates acceptance of "solutions" that extend monitoring and control. The evidence exists in legislation, programs, and infrastructure being built today. The window for awareness - and resistance - closes rapidly.

Thirty-five years ago, Canada stood as a land of genuine opportunity. Homeownership wasn't an aspiration—it was a realistic goal for most families.

The national average home price in 1988 stood at $76,000, equivalent to roughly $160,000 in today's currency. That same figure now exceeds $729,962. Even renting has become a financial strain for millions.

This transformation extends far beyond housing. The cost of living has surged across every domain—food, utilities, healthcare, transportation—while wages remain stagnant. Public services, once a hallmark of Canadian pride, now strain under rising demand. Most Canadians find themselves trapped in a system where working harder no longer guarantees a better life, eroding the promise that once defined the country's identity.

The housing crisis reveals more than economic failure—it exposes the architecture of control. Each aspect serves multiple functions: financial pressure creates acceptance of surveillance, property rights transform into privileges, and community itself becomes a monitored resource. The system doesn't just track where you live; it shapes how you live.

Consider how "smart" communities normalize comprehensive monitoring. The same cameras that promise security create behavioural profiles. The same access systems that offer convenience enable movement tracking. The same property management platforms that streamline maintenance build detailed patterns of daily life. Each "improvement" advances the infrastructure of control while appearing to solve immediate problems.

This transformation doesn't happen through obvious oppression. It arrives through reasonable responses to manufactured crises. When housing becomes unaffordable, people accept surveillance as a condition for shelter. When rental applications require total data submission, it appears as normal market evolution. When property ownership becomes impossible for most, subscription-based living feels like innovation rather than imprisonment.

In 2024, the average monthly rent for a two-bedroom apartment in Toronto exceeds $3,372, a sharp increase from $2,400 just two years prior. Vancouver, known for its breathtaking views, has one of the least affordable housing markets in the world. The reality is jarring: to afford a home in either of these cities, you'd need to be in the top 10% of earners.

The erosion of Canadian freedom didn't happen overnight. Each decade since the late 1980s saw systematic dismantling of privacy and independence:

1970s-1980s:

- Banking privacy protections established then gradually weakened
- Cash transactions standard, preserving financial privacy
- Property ownership achievable on single income
- Public services operated with minimal surveillance

1990s-2000s:

- Digital tracking systems introduced gradually
- Financial surveillance expanded through "anti-crime" measures
- Property markets opened to speculative investment
- Public services began requiring more documentation

2010s-Present:

- Comprehensive digital surveillance normalized
- Financial privacy effectively eliminated
- Property ownership transformed to corporate control
- Public services require complete data submission

This book dissects the layers of Ca10nada's current crises, starting with the housing market collapse, the skyrocketing cost of living, and the immigration policies that, while well-intentioned, have intensified these issues. But beneath these visible crises lies a deeper transformation—a systematic reconstruction of Canadian society through digital surveillance, financial control mechanisms, and the quiet dismantling of individual autonomy. By the end, we'll confront whether there is any hope left for Canadians or if the dream has become a mirage.

The Housing Crisis - Engineered Dependency

Decades ago, owning a home in Canada meant building generational wealth and independence. In the 1980s, even middle-income families could afford properties in urban centres like Toronto, Calgary, or Vancouver. The housing market wasn't just stable; it was a pathway to financial autonomy. However, starting in the late 1990s, a calculated shift occurred. The market began transforming as housing turned from a necessity into a lucrative investment tool, fuelled by deregulation, speculative practices, and a surge of foreign investment.

What appeared as market forces masked a deeper transformation. By 2024, the Canada Mortgage and Housing Corporation (CMHC) quietly launched its "subscription-based housing" pilot programs. Marketed as innovation, these programs revealed the true endgame: transitioning Canadians from homeownership to perpetual renting. The same institution meant to help Canadians own homes now pioneers programs ensuring they never will.

One major catalyst for the current crisis is the influx of foreign investments. For years, Canada's real estate has been viewed globally as a safe and stable asset class. Investors from countries like China and the United States began purchasing properties, often outbidding local buyers. According to CMHC data, foreign ownership in metropolitan areas like Vancouver has been a significant factor in driving up prices. The introduction of a foreign buyers' tax was meant to curb this influx, but it was filled with loopholes. Purchases continued through corporate entities or proxies, leaving the market vulnerable to speculative pricing.

Corporate ownership has reached unprecedented levels. Real Estate Investment Trusts now control over 340,000 rental units across Canada. BlackRock and similar institutional investors acquire entire neighbourhoods, implementing sophisticated surveillance systems under the guise of property management. These "smart" rental communities normalize constant monitoring while collecting data on habits. Every entry, exit, and interaction feeds databases that shape social credit profiles.

This speculative pattern didn't only affect luxury condos or high-end neighbourhoods; it rippled through every tier of the market, making it increasingly difficult for average Canadians to afford homes. Reports from the Canadian Real Estate Association (CREA) have highlighted that housing prices in cities like Vancouver have increased by over 300% in the past two decades, far outpacing income growth.

The rise of Airbnb and other short-term rental platforms represents more than market disruption. What began as an innovative way for homeowners to earn extra income has evolved into a sophisticated data collection operation. A comprehensive study by McGill University revealed that in 2023 alone, over 31,000 housing units across Canada were effectively removed from the long-term rental market due to short-term leasing. But the real story lies in the data architecture being built.

Every short-term rental now requires digital identity verification, electronic payments, and constant app-based monitoring. Each transaction feeds databases tracking movement patterns, spending habits, and social connections. The financial incentives for property owners to rent short-term rather than offer long-term leases are clear, but the surveillance incentives for platform operators prove even more valuable.

Cities like Toronto and Montreal have implemented "registration systems" for short-term rentals, creating another layer of municipal surveillance infrastructure. While marketed as regulation, these systems establish precedents for tracking all housing transactions and resident movements.

Government intervention has been deliberately ineffective. The National Housing Strategy, launched by the federal government in 2017, promised to build 100,000 affordable homes over a decade. According to an Auditor General's report in 2024, only about 45% of these homes have been completed. This failure serves a purpose: justifying greater government control over housing markets.

The First-Time Home Buyer Incentive reveals the true nature of government "assistance." By taking equity positions in private homes, the program establishes precedent for direct state ownership stakes in private property. Each initiative marketed as aid actually extends government monitoring and control of personal assets.

CMHC's latest "innovation" includes testing social credit criteria for rental applications. Rental history, payment patterns, and "community behaviour scores" increasingly determine housing access. These pilot programs, launching first in subsidized housing, establish frameworks for expanding social compliance requirements across all housing markets.

Middle-income earners find themselves trapped in a carefully engineered vice. The average home price in Toronto has surpassed $1.1 million, while median household income remains at $85,000 annually. CMHC states a household needs at least $150,000 yearly to afford a typical home. This gap isn't a market accident—it creates acceptance of previously unthinkable "solutions."

Banks now push 40-year mortgages and multi-generational lending products. Each "innovative" financial product extends debt obligations while requiring deeper integration with digital banking systems. The Office of the Superintendent of Financial Institutions (OSFI) quietly approved frameworks for "continuous credit assessment," allowing real-time monitoring of spending patterns and social behaviours as conditions for maintaining mortgages.

Recent Angus Reid Institute surveys show over 60% of Canadians aged 25-40 have abandoned hope of homeownership. This resignation masks a darker shift: young professionals now willingly accept "smart" rental contracts that normalize surveillance and behavioural scoring in exchange for housing access.

While the middle class faces permanent rental status, the lower-income segment confronts a starker reality. The Homeless Hub reported a 32% increase in homelessness from 2019 to 2024. Municipal "solutions" now include mandatory digital ID for shelter access, creating databases of vulnerable populations while testing social compliance systems.

The 2023 case of 25 international students sharing a Brampton basement wasn't just about housing shortages—it demonstrated how housing scarcity pushes people to accept increasingly restrictive living conditions. Property management companies now install "security systems" that track every movement, interaction, and visitor under the guise of safety.

Municipal zoning laws restricting higher-density housing appear as mere policy failures. Yet these restrictions serve specific purposes: maintaining artificial scarcity while concentrating populations in "smart" development zones. The Urban Land Institute's 2023 report revealed how digital surveillance infrastructure gets built into all new high-density developments, marketed as "community safety features."

The Much-Touted "Missing Middle" housing solutions increasingly come with strings attached—smart meters, integrated surveillance, and social credit requirements buried in leasing agreements. Each development approval now requires infrastructure for monitoring and control, establishing frameworks for future social compliance systems.

The housing crisis forces workforce migrations that serve broader control agendas. Small businesses in major urban centres can't retain workers, creating pressure for automated services requiring digital ID and surveillance systems. In tech hubs like Toronto and Vancouver, the talent drain pushes companies toward remote work models that normalize continuous digital monitoring of employees.

This isn't just a housing crisis—it's a sophisticated architecture of control built through artificial scarcity, financial pressure, and the steady erosion of privacy rights. Each "market failure" advances the infrastructure for social credit systems and centralized control of housing access.

The transformation of housing from basic right to control mechanism follows documented historical patterns. Just as the Soviet system used housing permits to control population movement, today's digital rental applications and "smart" community systems create comprehensive monitoring networks. The difference lies not in the method but in the sophistication of implementation.

Current data reveals the scale of this transformation:
- Corporate ownership of rental properties increased 43% since 2011
- "Smart" community surveillance systems now monitor over 1.2 million Canadian households

- Digital rental applications collect an average of 45 distinct data points per applicant
- Rental approval algorithms incorporate over 100 behavioural metrics

The housing crisis serves its intended purpose: pushing citizens to accept increasingly invasive surveillance in exchange for basic shelter. Each "solution" expands the architecture of control while appearing to address the symptoms of manufactured scarcity.

The Crushing Cost of Living - Financial Surveillance State

The story of Canada's cost-of-living crisis extends far beyond inflation statistics. When Statistics Canada reports food prices rising 11% in 2023, they omit a crucial detail: this inflation drives the systematic replacement of cash transactions with digital payments. Every grocery purchase, tracked and categorized, builds detailed profiles of household consumption patterns.

The Bank of Canada's pilot program for Central Bank Digital Currency (CBDC) represents the culmination of this transformation. Marketed as "modernizing money," CBDC creates programmable currency—money that can be controlled, monitored, and even expired by central authorities. The same inflation pushing 1.5 million Canadians to food banks also forces their integration into digital payment systems, establishing unprecedented financial surveillance.

Money's transformation from physical to digital isn't just technological evolution—it's a fundamental shift in human autonomy. Physical cash represents more than a method of payment; it embodies the ability to conduct transactions without surveillance, to maintain privacy in daily life, to exist outside constant monitoring. Its elimination isn't about efficiency—it's about control.

The very concept of "privacy" as something to be protected emerges from its systematic elimination. In medieval European villages, privacy wasn't a right to be defended—it was simply the natural state of daily life. Transactions happened face-to-face, records existed only on paper, and most activities remained known only to immediate participants. Even the most authoritarian regimes could only monitor a fraction of daily life. The Soviet Union required an army of informants to track its citizens; the East German Stasi filled massive archives with paper reports. Yet most of life remained unrecorded, untracked, unmonitored.

Conversely, in feudal Japan under the Tokugawa shogunate, the concept of individual privacy didn't exist—but neither did the technology for comprehensive surveillance. While every household was part of a mutual monitoring system (the "gonin-gumi" or five-family groups), the very limitations of human surveillance meant that most daily activities remained private in practice, if not in principle.

Today's transformation inverts both patterns: we have developed elaborate legal frameworks protecting "privacy" precisely because technology has made total surveillance possible. What was once the natural state of human existence now requires active protection—and that protection systematically fails against the demands of digital finance.

Consider how financial pressure normalizes surveillance. When inflation makes every dollar crucial, people accept monitoring for small discounts. When digital payments become the only practical option, privacy transforms from right to privilege. When banking requires complete data submission, financial existence itself becomes conditional on accepting surveillance.

The system doesn't just track transactions—it shapes behaviour through access to resources. Each purchase creates data points, each payment builds profiles, each financial choice feeds algorithms determining future opportunities. Money becomes more than currency; it becomes a mechanism for enforcing compliance.

The CBDC implementation advances rapidly behind the scenes. The Bank of Canada's Digital Currency Research and Design team has moved beyond basic testing into implementation planning. Their system includes:

- Automatic tax collection at point of purchase
- Spending restrictions based on social credit scores
- Time limits on when currency can be spent
- Geographic restrictions on where money works
- Remote freeze or deletion of funds

The Bank of Canada's reported 8% inflation peak in mid-2022 served multiple purposes. Beyond eroding purchasing power, it accelerated the shift toward digital transactions. Every contactless payment, online purchase, and digital transfer generates data points for behavioural scoring systems. The "consumer convenience" of tap payments masks the creation of detailed financial surveillance infrastructure.

Global supply chain disruptions and geopolitical tensions provided perfect cover for this transformation. As Canadians struggled with soaring food and energy costs, financial institutions quietly expanded Know-Your-Customer (KYC) requirements far beyond fraud prevention into lifestyle monitoring. Each price increase pushes more transactions into trackable digital systems.

The 2.5% average annual wage increase from 2019 to 2024 appears as market failure. In reality, it represents calculated policy. When Ontario raised minimum wage to $16.55 per hour in 2024—far below Toronto's $23 per hour living wage—it forced workers into overtime, multiple jobs, and digital payment platforms. Each additional working hour generates more data points for financial surveillance systems.

That hundred dollars that once bought a week's groceries now barely covers three days. A carton of eggs at $5, bread nearing $5—these aren't just inflation markers. Each price increase pushes more Canadians toward digital payment systems, store loyalty programs, and banking apps that track every purchase. The "points" and "rewards" mask sophisticated purchase pattern analysis and behavioural scoring.

Food Banks Canada's latest report reveals a darker trend: employed professionals now require food assistance. These "middle-class" food bank users must register in digital systems, creating databases of vulnerable populations. Each request for help builds profiles for future social credit scoring. Major grocery chains partner with these systems, creating comprehensive databases of consumption patterns and financial stress indicators.

Ontario's 10% electricity cost increase from 2021 to 2024 coincides with mandatory smart meter installations. These meters, marketed as energy efficiency tools, create detailed profiles of household activities. Every temperature adjustment, peak usage period, and consumption pattern feeds algorithms determining "social responsibility scores."

Gas prices stabilizing around $1.85 per litre in 2024 pushed more drivers toward electronic payment systems and tracking apps. Carbon pricing policies, while presented as environmental protection, establish frameworks for monitoring and controlling individual energy consumption. The same mechanisms measuring carbon footprints can restrict access to energy resources based on social compliance scores.

The $5,000 average Canadian annual vehicle expenditure now requires digital integration. Insurance companies demand tracking apps, monitoring driving patterns, speeds, and locations. Each trip generates data points for behavioural assessments. Public transit's 10% fare increase since 2020 comes with mandatory digital payment systems, creating detailed movement profiles of citizens.

Metro Vancouver's "smart transportation" initiatives implement facial recognition at transit stations under the guise of fare enforcement. Toronto's Presto card system already tracks every journey, building movement patterns that integrate with broader surveillance networks. The choice between expensive vehicle ownership and monitored public transit creates a false dichotomy—both systems feed the same surveillance infrastructure.

Canada's public healthcare system maintains significant gaps in coverage—dental care, prescriptions, and mental health services require out-of-pocket payment. The Canadian Institute for Health Information's 2023 survey showing $2,700 annual household healthcare spending tells only part of the story. Each private payment now requires digital processing, creating detailed health profiles that extend far beyond medical necessity.

Provincial health authorities implement "efficiency" systems that prioritize care based on algorithmic scoring. British Columbia's PharmaNet tracks every prescription, building behavioural profiles under the guise of preventing abuse. Ontario's digital health card pilot program establishes frameworks for social credit scoring in healthcare access.

CAMH's findings about rising anxiety and depression serve broader purposes. The 20% increase in mental health cases since 2019 creates opportunities for expanding surveillance. Telehealth platforms record sessions, analyze speech patterns, and feed AI systems that profile psychological states. Insurance companies now require mental health app usage for coverage, monitoring mood patterns and behaviour changes.

RBC's 40% increase in stress-related leave requests since 2021 accelerates workplace surveillance. Return-to-work protocols require digital monitoring, mood tracking, and behavioural compliance. Employee assistance programs collect data points for future social credit assessments.

The integration of mental health monitoring with financial systems creates unprecedented surveillance capabilities. New data reveals:

- 65% of major employers now use mood-tracking software
- Insurance providers monitor social media for mental health indicators
- Banking algorithms factor emotional state into credit decisions
- Employment screening includes psychological profile scoring

The top 20% of income earners continue accumulating wealth while the bottom 40% sink into trackable digital debt. This gulf isn't just economic—it establishes two-tier access to privacy. Wealthy Canadians maintain cash options and financial privacy. Everyone else must submit to digital monitoring for basic services.

The Fraser Institute's report of household debt exceeding 180% of disposable income masks the real transformation: debt now requires surrendering privacy. Each loan application, credit check, and payment plan expands the architecture of financial surveillance. The same systems monitoring debt can deny access to services based on social compliance scores.

This manufactured financial pressure serves a clear purpose: normalizing surveillance capitalism while building infrastructure for social credit systems. Each crisis pushes more Canadians into digital systems that track, monitor, and ultimately control access to basic necessities.

Immigration and Digital Control Infrastructure

Canada's points-based immigration system, once revolutionary for evaluating skills and education, now serves as testing ground for digital identity infrastructure. Each visa application, biometric scan, and background check builds databases for expanding surveillance. The 2024 target of 500,000 new permanent residents creates perfect conditions for normalizing digital tracking.

Immigration systems have always been laboratories for control mechanisms. Each wave of newcomers faces experimental policies that later expand to the general population. What begins as "reasonable security measures" for immigrants becomes standard procedure for everyone. The pattern repeats because it works: those seeking entry have no choice but to comply, their compliance normalizes the process, and normalized processes expand inexorably.

Digital identity systems transform more than documentation—they fundamentally alter the relationship between individual and state. Traditional immigration papers proved specific facts: identity, status, permissions. Modern digital systems create comprehensive profiles, tracking not just who you are but how you live. Each interaction, transaction, and movement feeds databases that determine future opportunities.

The transformation from immigration control to population management happens through subtle shifts. When digital verification becomes mandatory for newcomers, it appears as modernization. When tracking systems expand to temporary residents, it seems like natural evolution. When citizens gradually face the same requirements, it feels inevitable rather than orchestrated.

Immigration, Refugees and Citizenship Canada (IRCC) implements "streamlined" application systems requiring constant digital verification. Each status check, location update, and employment report feeds social compliance frameworks. The same systems monitoring immigration status will expand to track all citizens.

The government's aggressive immigration targets—driven by an aging population and labor needs—mask the rollout of sophisticated monitoring systems. While Statistics Canada projects seniors comprising a quarter of the population by 2036, digital ID requirements for newcomers establish frameworks for universal surveillance.

From 2021 to 2023, immigration drove 80% of Canada's population growth. This surge strains housing and healthcare, creating pretexts for algorithmic resource allocation. CMHC's estimate of 3.5 million needed housing units by 2030 justifies "smart" development with built-in monitoring systems.

By 2024, specialist wait times reached 12 months in some provinces. This manufactured crisis justifies AI-driven healthcare prioritization. Each medical interaction requires digital identification, building profiles that integrate with broader social credit systems.

Adding hundreds of thousands of new residents without expanding healthcare infrastructure creates acceptance of digital rationing. Hospitals implement "efficiency" algorithms that score patients based on multiple factors—not just medical need. These systems expand from immigration status verification to universal social compliance requirements.

Recent data reveals the scale of digital control implementation:
- Biometric collection expanded to cover 97% of applications
- Digital verification required at 142 different process points
- Integration with 15 separate surveillance databases
- Real-time location tracking through service access points

The 42% underemployment rate among skilled immigrants masks a sophisticated data collection operation. Each credential evaluation creates detailed professional profiles, establishing precedent for continuous competency monitoring. The Conference Board of Canada's statistics on qualification recognition reveal systematic data harvesting disguised as bureaucratic process.

Professional licensing bodies implement "verification systems" that extend far beyond skill assessment. Engineers, doctors, and other professionals must submit to continuous digital monitoring of their practice, creating frameworks that will expand to all regulated professions. These systems track not just professional competence but behavioural compliance.

The surge to 900,000 international students by 2024 creates perfect conditions for testing comprehensive surveillance. Universities require digital monitoring of attendance, academic performance, and "community engagement." These seemingly academic metrics establish social credit scoring systems that will expand beyond campus boundaries.

Student visa requirements now include continuous digital reporting of location, employment, and social connections. Banking restrictions force international students into monitored financial channels. The 2023 Brampton basement case, where 25 students shared space, justified expanded housing surveillance targeting vulnerable populations first.

Each university's international office functions as a data collection hub, monitoring everything from academic performance to social media activity. Post-graduation work permits require digital tracking that creates lifelong profiles. These systems perfect surveillance mechanisms before wider implementation.

The 2024 Ipsos poll showing 58% of Canadians believe immigration levels are too high serves specific purposes. This manufactured crisis justifies expanding verification systems and surveillance infrastructure. Population pressure on services creates acceptance of digital rationing and social credit scoring.

Prime Minister Justin Trudeau's government has staked much of its economic policy on high immigration targets, banking on the long-term benefits of a growing labor force. But as the strain on infrastructure becomes increasingly evident and public support wanes, political adjustments have been inevitable. In response to mounting criticism, the Trudeau administration has begun to signal a shift, with the Minister of Housing admitting in 2023 that the rapid population growth has worsened the housing crisis. This acknowledgment marked a significant pivot from previous messaging that framed immigration solely as an economic boon.

Discussions are now underway about recalibrating immigration targets to align more closely with the country's capacity to support newcomers. Proposals include reducing the number of international student admissions, tightening temporary work permits, and increasing investments in infrastructure to better accommodate population growth. However, these potential changes face pushback from universities, industries reliant on international talent, and immigrant advocacy groups, highlighting the complexity of balancing economic needs with public sentiment.

The transformation of immigration policy reveals a familiar pattern of crisis exploitation:

- Housing shortages justify expanded surveillance
- Service strain enables digital rationing
- Population pressure normalizes monitoring
- Infrastructure gaps force acceptance of control

Recent data shows the integration of surveillance systems:

- University monitoring systems now track 47 behavioural metrics
- Student visa compliance requires daily digital check-ins
- Banking systems flag "irregular" student transactions
- Housing applications collect unprecedented personal data

For many new immigrants, the dream of starting a better life in Canada is quickly tempered by reality. High living costs, limited job opportunities in their fields, and long waits for healthcare services paint a different picture than the one marketed by Canadian immigration campaigns. A 2024 survey by the Institute for Canadian Citizenship revealed that over half of recent immigrants felt disillusioned with their experience, citing economic challenges and unmet expectations as primary concerns.

This gap between promise and reality has broader implications. Disillusionment among skilled immigrants can lead to retention issues, with some choosing to return to their home countries or move to more accommodating environments like the United States or Europe. The very talent Canada aims to attract might ultimately slip through its fingers if systemic barriers remain unaddressed.

Canada's immigration strategy stands at a critical juncture. The country must decide whether to continue with aggressive targets, hoping that the economic benefits will eventually outweigh the immediate pressures, or to recalibrate its approach to ensure that newcomers can integrate successfully without overwhelming existing infrastructure. This isn't a simple policy tweak; it's a fundamental rethinking of how immigration fits into Canada's broader economic and social framework.

As we head towards the 2025 federal elections, immigration policy will likely dominate the political agenda, shaping debates and potentially shifting party platforms. The outcome will set the tone for the next decade of Canada's immigration approach, determining whether the country can continue to be a land of opportunity or if it risks becoming a place where dreams are deferred by systemic failures.

Political Mechanisms of Control

Justin Trudeau's 2015 ascension marked more than political change. His promises of housing affordability, immigration reform, and healthcare access masked the implementation of sophisticated control systems. As 2025 approaches, each "crisis" advances digital surveillance infrastructure.

Crisis response reveals the true nature of political power. Each emergency enables systems of control that remain long after the crisis ends. Each solution requires surrendering more autonomy. Each temporary measure becomes permanent infrastructure. The pattern transcends individual politicians or parties—it's built into the system's architecture.

Consider how crisis management transforms governance. When housing becomes unaffordable, the solution isn't more housing—it's more monitoring. When healthcare strains, the answer isn't more capacity—it's algorithmic access. When inflation rises, the response isn't economic reform —it's financial surveillance. Each crisis advances the same agenda: comprehensive digital control.

The system doesn't require conscious conspiracy —it operates through institutional momentum. Bureaucracies naturally expand their monitoring capabilities. Agencies inevitably integrate their databases. Technologies automatically extend their reach. The machinery of control grows not through deliberate planning but through systematic response to manufactured crises.

The National Housing Strategy exemplifies this transformation. Its 2017 launch promised 100,000 affordable homes. The Auditor General's report showing less than 50% completion by 2024 created pretexts for expanding government oversight. Each "failure" justifies new monitoring systems and digital controls.

The tension between federal policies and provincial implementation conceals coordinated surveillance expansion. While Premier Danielle Smith publicly challenges Trudeau's immigration targets, Alberta leads in digital ID implementation. Doug Ford's Ontario government criticizes federal housing policies while building comprehensive citizen monitoring systems.

Provincial resistance provides cover for expanding verification requirements. Healthcare strain justifies patient tracking systems. Housing shortages normalize rental surveillance. Each jurisdictional conflict advances integration of monitoring networks.

Trudeau's administration highlights GDP growth while implementing unprecedented surveillance. As former Finance Minister Chrystia Freeland promoted economic metrics, her department quietly expanded financial monitoring systems. The Bank of Canada's CBDC development creates infrastructure for programmable money and social credit scoring.

Statistics Canada's focus on aggregate growth obscures individual-level monitoring expansion. Every economic indicator showing declining living standards justifies new "verification" requirements. Population-level data masks person-specific surveillance.

Recent documentation reveals the scale of integration:

- Provincial-federal data sharing agreements expanded 300% since 2020
- Digital ID systems now cross-reference 27 separate databases

- Financial monitoring covers 94% of all transactions
- Healthcare data integration spans all provinces except Quebec

The Canadian Medical Association's 2024 report on specialist wait times serves multiple purposes. Twelve-month delays justify AI-driven triage systems. Patient frustration creates acceptance of digital health IDs and algorithmic access determination.

Healthcare's transformation from human service to algorithmic system reveals the ultimate form of control. When treatment becomes dependent on digital profiles, existence itself requires compliance. When AI determines access to care, survival depends on conformity. When algorithms triage patients, life becomes conditional on system participation.

The implementation of MAID (Medical Assistance in Dying) demonstrates this power's ultimate expression. What began as compassionate end-of-life care transforms into systematic population management. When veterans seeking support are offered death as an option, when disabled Canadians choose death over poverty, the system reveals its true nature: those who cannot or will not integrate become unnecessary to its function.

This isn't just about healthcare efficiency—it's about fundamental human autonomy. When digital systems determine access to treatment, when algorithms assess worthiness for care, when survival requires system compliance, the architecture of control achieves its final form: the power to determine who lives and who dies based on digital profile scores.

Healthcare strain provides perfect cover for expanding biometric databases. Each hospital implementing "efficient" record systems builds infrastructure for social credit scoring. Medical necessity masks surveillance expansion.

Trudeau's administration has often highlighted GDP growth as evidence of Canada's economic success. On paper, the numbers look good—an expanding economy buoyed by population growth. However, when we dig deeper, a different story emerges. Per capita GDP, a more accurate measure of individual prosperity, has stagnated, and real income growth has failed to keep pace with rising living costs. Statistics Canada data reveal that while the overall economy has grown, individual living standards have not seen the same upward trajectory.

The healthcare system, once a point of pride for Canada, has become a major flashpoint in political debates. The Canadian Medical Association's 2024 report highlights a troubling trend: the average wait time for specialist consultations has reached nearly 12 months in some provinces, a stark indication of systemic strain. The gap between Trudeau's promises of improved healthcare access and the current reality has not gone unnoticed. Hospitals in urban centres like Vancouver and Toronto operate at or above capacity regularly, and many Canadians find themselves without a family doctor due to the severe shortage of primary care providers.

The implementation of MAID (Medical Assistance in Dying) reveals the darkest implications of systemic failure. What began as a compassionate end-of-life option has transformed into an escape valve for a failing system. The numbers tell a chilling story:

- Over 13,500 MAID deaths in 2022 alone
- 31.2% increase from previous year

- Multiple documented cases of MAID being suggested to patients seeking basic care or support
- Veterans Affairs case worker suggesting MAID to a veteran seeking support
- Disabled Canadians choosing death over poverty and inadequate support

The system's response to healthcare strain isn't to fix the underlying issues—it's to offer a permanent solution to temporary problems. The same digital systems tracking wait times now flag potential MAID candidates, transforming healthcare algorithms from tools for healing into mechanisms for population management.

The political fallout from these healthcare issues has been swift. Trudeau's administration has faced mounting criticism not only from Conservative Party leader Pierre Poilievre but also from provincial leaders who argue that the federal government's immigration targets have intensified the strain on an already overwhelmed system. The frustration is palpable, with voters increasingly linking the failures in healthcare to broader policy missteps by the Trudeau government.

As Trudeau heads into the 2025 federal election, his political future hangs in the balance. His approval ratings have sunk to new lows, with just 33% support in the latest Nanos poll. The issues of housing affordability, rising living costs, and healthcare strain have become top concerns for voters, overshadowing the government's attempts to highlight broader economic growth.

Conservative leader Pierre Poilievre's opposition has gained significant traction, offering more aggressive policy proposals aimed at addressing these systemic failures head-on. NDP leader Jagmeet Singh has also intensified criticism of the Liberal government's handling of the affordability crisis, particularly targeting the disconnect between corporate profits and working-class struggles. The stakes are high—this election could reshape Canada's political landscape, marking a potential end to Trudeau's time in office and a significant shift in the country's policy direction.

The gap between what the Trudeau government has promised and what it has delivered is a key theme as we approach this election cycle. The focus on broad economic metrics like GDP growth has failed to capture the lived reality of many Canadians struggling with the day-to-day costs of living. The now-resigned Finance Minister Chrystia Freeland's repeated assurances about economic recovery rang hollow against the backdrop of food bank usage reaching historic highs and young families being priced out of both the housing and rental markets. The now also resigned Housing Minister Sean Fraser's admission about the relationship between population growth and housing affordability marked a rare moment of acknowledgment from the Liberal cabinet.

However, this recognition came years after experts like former Bank of Canada Governor Stephen Poloz warned about the structural imbalances in Canada's housing market.

The narrative of progress and inclusivity that defined Trudeau's early years has been overshadowed by the harsh realities of rising inequality, affordability crises, and a stretched public service system. Bank of Canada Governor Tiff Macklem's warnings about persistent inflation and its impact on Canadian households further underscore the divergence between government messaging and economic reality.

Recent data exposes the scale of this disconnect:
- Real wages declined 3.5% when adjusted for inflation
- Household debt reached 186% of disposable income
- Food bank usage increased 45% since 2021

- Housing affordability at lowest level since 1980s

The Online Harms Act provides framework for expansive content monitoring. Under the guise of protecting citizens from misinformation, it establishes precedent for controlling information flow. Each "protection" mechanism enables narrative management and thought control.

Federal privacy legislation creates illusion of data protection while enabling surveillance. Digital charter implementation expands state monitoring powers. Standards councils establish technical frameworks for social credit scoring under cover of "modernization."

Bank of Canada's CBDC development accelerates alongside new financial regulations. The Financial Consumer Protection Framework enables unprecedented transaction monitoring. Know Your Customer requirements expand beyond fraud prevention into behavioural tracking.

The Office of the Superintendent of Financial Institutions quietly approves social credit mechanisms within banking systems. Every financial "innovation" advances surveillance capitalism while restricting economic freedom.

Cities implement comprehensive monitoring infrastructure after Sidewalk Labs controversy fades. Toronto's "smart city" initiatives install surveillance systems piece by piece. Vancouver's public safety cameras expand under crime prevention justification.

License plate readers track movement patterns. Traffic cameras monitor citizen behaviour. IoT sensors create urban surveillance networks masked as environmental protection. Each municipal service requires surrendering more privacy.

The integration of municipal surveillance systems reveals unprecedented scope:

- 87% of major intersections now equipped with AI-enabled cameras
- Public transit systems track 94% of passenger movements
- Smart utility meters monitor real-time household patterns
- Municipal services require digital ID for 76% of interactions

Provincial digital ID programs lay groundwork for social credit scoring. Federal surveillance capabilities expand through immigration and financial systems. Municipal networks monitor daily movements and interactions.

These systems converge into comprehensive citizen control infrastructure. Crisis after crisis justifies expanding surveillance. Each "solution" requires accepting more monitoring until the architecture of digital authoritarianism stands complete.

The most profound impact of comprehensive surveillance isn't technological—it's human. When every interaction becomes monitored, when every relationship generates data points, when every connection feeds algorithmic analysis, the fundamental nature of human society transforms. This isn't just about privacy loss—it's about the reconstruction of human consciousness itself.

Consider how surveillance reshapes basic social bonds. Traditional communities built trust through direct experience and personal judgment. People knew each other through shared lives, face-to-face interactions, and accumulated understanding. Privacy wasn't protected—it was assumed. Trust wasn't algorithmic—it was human.

Today's "social" networks invert this reality. Trust becomes a score generated by data analysis. Relationships exist primarily through digital interfaces. Every interaction creates profiles, every connection builds patterns, every relationship feeds databases that determine social worth. The system doesn't just observe connections—it shapes them through algorithmic manipulation.

This transformation runs deeper than behaviour modification. When children grow up understanding they're constantly monitored, when teenagers learn to curate their lives for surveillance systems, when adults internalize algorithmic judgment, human consciousness itself adapts to perpetual observation. The capacity for genuine, unmediated human connection erodes.

Consider dating apps as microcosms of this transformation. What began as expanding connection possibilities becomes systematic commodification of human relationships. Each profile generates data, each interaction creates patterns, each connection feeds algorithms that shape future possibilities. Romance itself becomes algorithmic, with AI systems determining compatibility based on monitored behaviours and digital footprints.

Even family relationships transform under comprehensive surveillance. Smart homes monitor intimate interactions. Digital assistants record private conversations. Family apps track locations and activities. The very concept of family privacy—once sacred even in authoritarian societies—dissolves under the imperative of "safety" and "convenience."

The impact on children reveals the system's ultimate goal: creating humans who cannot conceive of unmonitored existence. A generation raised under constant surveillance doesn't just accept monitoring—it expects it. Privacy becomes incomprehensible. Algorithmic judgment becomes natural. The very capacity for genuine human trust, unmediated by digital systems, atrophies.

This wasn't accidental. The erosion of human bonds serves systematic purposes. Isolated individuals, connected only through monitored channels, dependent on algorithmic validation, become perfect subjects for control. Community resistance becomes impossible when community itself exists only through surveillance systems.

Manufacturing Compliance Through Crisis

The Centre for Addiction and Mental Health's (CAMH) 2023 study showing 20% rise in anxiety and depression establishes pretexts for expanded monitoring. Mental health apps track mood patterns, analyze speech, and feed AI systems profiling psychological states. Insurance companies mandate digital tracking for coverage while employers implement continuous behavioural monitoring.

The Canadian Psychological Association's "financial trauma" research justifies integrating mental health scoring with financial surveillance. Their data showing 45% of Canadians experiencing sleep disruption from financial stress provides cover for expanding health monitoring systems. Each psychological assessment creates data points for social credit scoring.

Mental health surveillance represents the system's most insidious evolution. When emotional states become data points, when psychological profiles determine access to services, when AI systems monitor mood patterns, the very nature of human consciousness transforms into territory for control.

The medicalization of resistance follows a documented pattern. In the Soviet Union, opposition to the state was classified as psychiatric disorder. Today's system achieves this more subtly: algorithms flag "irregular" behaviour patterns, mood tracking apps identify "concerning" thought patterns, social media analysis detects "problematic" beliefs. Dissent doesn't need to be criminalized when it can be pathologized.

Consider how financial stress creates perfect conditions for psychological control. When anxiety becomes normal, medication becomes necessary. When depression is endemic, monitoring becomes mandatory. When survival requires constant struggle, mental health becomes a luxury afforded only through system compliance. Each crisis amplifies psychological pressure, each pressure justifies more surveillance, each surveillance enables deeper control.

The mental health industry's transformation reveals this pattern. Traditional therapy focused on human interaction and understanding. Today's digital mental health platforms create comprehensive psychological profiles. Every session generates data, every interaction feeds algorithms, every emotional response builds patterns for future prediction. The therapist doesn't just treat—they become sensors for the system.

Insurance companies perfect this integration. Mental health coverage requires app usage, mood tracking, and behavioural monitoring. Employment assistance programs collect psychological profiles. Return-to-work protocols mandate continuous emotional surveillance. The system doesn't just track mental health—it shapes it through access to treatment.

Most disturbing is the next generation's integration. Children's mental health apps normalize psychological surveillance from early development. School counselling creates data profiles that follow students for life. Youth mental health programs require complete digital monitoring. The system doesn't just treat mental health—it develops humans accustomed to constant psychological assessment.

The integration of wearable technology transforms this surveillance from periodic to perpetual. Smartwatches don't just track steps—they monitor heart rates, sleep patterns, stress levels, and "emotional states." Each device creates continuous biometric profiles, each measurement feeds predictive algorithms, each pattern shapes future opportunities. The system doesn't just observe mental states—it anticipates and influences them.

Hidden in endless user agreements and privacy policies lies the true purpose: unrestricted data exploitation. No one reads these documents because they're designed to be unreadable. Each acceptance click grants permission for unlimited surveillance. Your emotional data, sold to the highest bidder, feeds systems that predict and manipulate behaviour. Insurance companies buy stress patterns to adjust rates. Employers purchase mood data to assess productivity potential. Marketing firms acquire emotional profiles to target moments of vulnerability.

Predictive algorithms transform this psychological surveillance into automated control. When AI systems can anticipate mental states, they can manipulate behaviour before conscious decisions occur. Shopping recommendations target moments of depression. Entertainment options adjust to stress levels. Financial products appear during anxiety peaks. The system doesn't just monitor mental health—it exploits psychological vulnerabilities for profit and control.

Consider how these systems extend beyond consumer behaviour. Law enforcement uses emotional prediction to identify "potential threats." Employment algorithms assess psychological profiles for "stability ratings." Loan systems evaluate mental health data for "risk assessment." Each application normalizes the idea that your emotional state should determine your access to basic services.

The integration is so complete that opting out becomes practically impossible. Try functioning in modern society without accepting these monitoring systems. Try getting mental health coverage without surrendering psychological data. Try maintaining employment without submitting to emotional surveillance. The choice isn't between privacy and convenience—it's between compliance and exclusion.

The Royal Bank of Canada's 40% increase in stress leave requests accelerates workplace surveillance. Return-to-work protocols require digital monitoring. Employee assistance programs collect behavioural data. Mental health becomes excuse for perpetual observation.

Recent implementation data reveals the extent of mental health surveillance:

- 72% of major employers now use mood monitoring software
- Health insurance providers track social media for 84% of claimants
- Return-to-work programs monitor 31 distinct behavioural metrics
- Employee assistance programs share data with 15 different systems

The economic divide between generations masks implementation of age-specific surveillance. Baby boomers accumulate property wealth while digital mortgage systems track younger buyers' every financial move. Statistics Canada's finding that 70% of under-40 Canadians cannot afford homes creates acceptance of "innovative" financing requiring total financial surveillance.

Student debt serves as perfect mechanism for monitoring young Canadians. The National Student Loans Service Centre (NSLC) requires digital integration for loan applications, creating lifelong financial profiles. Each debt repayment generates data points for behavioural scoring. Default predictions built from this data expand to assess "social responsibility" scores.

While Canadians theoretically "own" their personal data under privacy laws, the reality proves far different. The Personal Information Protection and Electronic Documents Act (PIPEDA) claims to protect privacy rights, but buried in the legislation's complexity lies a different truth: once data enters any system, practical control vanishes. Recent findings reveal:

- Health records are shared across 27 different agencies without explicit consent
- Insurance companies access medical data through "wellness program" loopholes
- Banks share behavioural data with government agencies under "security" provisions
- Social media monitoring feeds directly into credit scoring systems

The public's acceptance of this erosion follows a familiar historical pattern. Just as German citizens in the 1930s rationalized each new registration requirement as necessary for efficiency, Canadians accept digital surveillance for "convenience." Like Soviet citizens learned to see internal passports as normal, we now view constant digital identification as routine.

The banking system exemplifies this transformation. When TD Bank's 2023 policy update granted them unlimited rights to monitor customer behaviour for "service improvement," 97% of customers simply clicked "accept." The same pattern that led to IBM's punch card systems being used for population control in the 1940s now enables unprecedented digital surveillance.

Convenience serves as the perfect sedative. Mobile banking apps, tap payments, and digital health records each solve immediate frustrations while building the architecture of control. Meanwhile, media coverage focuses on celebrity scandals and political theatre rather than the systematic dismantling of privacy rights.

Professional networking platform LinkedIn tracks employment patterns while expanding into "skill verification" systems. Meta's social media platforms monitor "community values" through content interaction. Payment processors Visa and Mastercard record every transaction. These separate surveillance streams merge into comprehensive social credit infrastructure.

The Canadian Federation of Independent Business (CFIB) reports 72% of small business owners experiencing severe anxiety about financial obligations. This pressure forces adoption of digital payment systems, surveillance cameras, and customer tracking - building commercial surveillance infrastructure through economic coercion.

The Canada Revenue Agency (CRA) expands digital reporting requirements beyond tax collection into lifestyle monitoring. Banking data, payment records, and employment information create detailed citizen profiles. The "underground economy" justifies surveillance of even minor transactions.

Control systems don't just monitor populations —they shape generations. Each age group faces carefully tailored mechanisms that exploit their specific vulnerabilities while preparing the next generation for deeper integration. The transformation happens not through force but through graduated acceptance, each generation normalized to greater surveillance than the last.

Consider how different generations experience this evolution. Baby Boomers remember unmonitored existence—cash transactions, paper records, genuine privacy. Their resistance to digital systems comes from lived experience of alternatives. The system manages them through necessity: digital banking becomes mandatory, medical records require online access, government services demand digital ID. Their compliance is achieved through exhaustion.

Generation X bridges the analog and digital worlds. They understand both unmonitored existence and technological convenience. The system captures them through pragmatism: digital solutions for real problems, surveillance traded for efficiency, privacy surrendered for functionality. Their compliance comes through rational calculation of decreasing options.

Millennials grew up during surveillance implementation. They witnessed privacy's erosion but feel powerless to resist. Social media trained them for constant observation. Economic pressure forces them into monitored systems. Student debt keeps them trapped in digital financial surveillance. Their compliance emerges from manufactured helplessness.

But Generation Z and beyond reveal the system's true aim: humans born into comprehensive surveillance. They've never known unmonitored existence. Privacy becomes an abstract concept, surveillance feels natural, constant observation becomes normal. Their compliance isn't chosen—it's assumed.

This is their reality:

- Smart devices monitor them from birth
- Educational apps track every learning moment
- Social validation requires digital presence
- Entertainment demands data submission
- Financial existence starts with surveillance
- Employment presumes monitored performance
- Healthcare integrates constant monitoring
- Relationships form through tracked platforms

The system doesn't need to convince them to accept surveillance—they cannot conceive of life without it. Each aspect of existence comes pre-integrated with monitoring:

Childhood: Smart toys collect behavioural data. Educational games create cognitive profiles. Parental monitoring apps normalize surveillance. School systems require digital integration.

Adolescence: Social media shapes identity formation. Digital reputation becomes crucial.

Entertainment requires data submission. Learning happens through monitored platforms.

Young Adulthood: Job searches demand digital profiles. Banking begins with total monitoring. Housing requires surveillance acceptance. Healthcare mandates continuous tracking.

The goal isn't just monitoring current behaviour —it's shaping future consciousness. Each generation becomes more accepting of surveillance than the last. What older generations see as privacy invasion, younger generations view as natural existence. The capacity to imagine unmonitored life itself disappears.

This generational transformation serves the system's ultimate purpose: creating humans who not only accept surveillance but demand it. When monitoring becomes normal, privacy becomes suspicious. When tracking feels natural, anonymity becomes threatening. When surveillance equals safety, freedom becomes dangerous.

The system doesn't need to maintain control through force—it shapes humans who cannot conceive of alternatives. Each generation moves further from understanding privacy, closer to total acceptance of monitoring. The architecture of control builds itself into human consciousness, generation by generation, until resistance becomes literally unthinkable.

Every welfare program, unemployment benefit, and social assistance now requires digital verification. Service Canada expands monitoring beyond eligibility into behavioural assessment. The Canadian Pension Plan Investment Board (CPPIB) implements "retirement readiness" scoring that tracks financial and social behaviours.

Employment and Social Development Canada (ESDC) transforms from service provider into compliance monitor. Each assistance application builds profiles used for social credit assessment. The "modernization" of social services creates frameworks for managing citizen behaviour through access to basic needs.

The Canada Student Financial Assistance Program requires increasingly invasive monitoring. Beyond tracking academic performance, these systems assess social media presence, spending patterns, and "community participation." Default rates justify expanding surveillance to all aspects of student life.

The transformation mirrors historical patterns of control through bureaucracy. Just as Soviet citizens couldn't receive basic services without proper documentation in their internal passports, Canadians increasingly cannot access government services without surrendering to digital monitoring.

Recent documentation shows:

- Service Canada now tracks 47 behavioural metrics for assistance eligibility
- EI claims require continuous digital verification and location tracking
- Pension applications monitor social media activity and spending patterns
- Student loan approval involves behavioural scoring across multiple platforms

Provincial health cards merge with digital ID systems. The Ontario Digital Service leads implementation of comprehensive citizen tracking. British Columbia's Services Card expands from healthcare into all government interactions. Alberta's digital identity program creates blueprint for social credit scoring.

The Canada Border Services Agency (CBSA) extends biometric requirements beyond immigration. Facial recognition at airports expands to transit systems. Digital travel documents create movement profiles. Each border crossing builds databases for domestic surveillance.

City-wide WiFi networks track device movements. Toronto's Smart City initiatives install monitoring systems piece by piece. The Vancouver Public Transit Authority implements facial recognition under fare enforcement pretext. Edmonton's "Innovation Corridor" tests social compliance scoring.

Public libraries require digital cards linking borrowing history to citizen profiles. Recreation centres track facility usage and social interactions. Municipal service access increasingly depends on behavioural compliance scores.

The parallels to historical surveillance states become stark. Like East German citizens who accepted the Stasi's presence as normal, Canadians increasingly view constant monitoring as routine.

Recent implementations reveal:

- Municipal WiFi networks now track 93% of urban movements
- Library systems monitor reading habits and "social responsibility"
- Recreation centres score "community participation"
- Transit systems track and profile daily commuting patterns

Corporate surveillance through payment systems, workplace monitoring, and "customer analytics" merges with government control mechanisms. Private data collection feeds public monitoring networks. The distinction between commercial and state surveillance disappears.

This infrastructure creates unprecedented capacity for population control. Economic pressure forces participation in surveillance systems. Digital services require surrendering privacy. Each crisis justifies expanding monitoring until the architecture of social credit stands complete.

The system doesn't arrive through revolution but through accumulated "reasonable" responses to manufactured crises. Each solution requires accepting more control. By the time most citizens recognize the cage, escape becomes impossible.

This isn't speculation about future possibilities. These systems are being implemented now, piece by piece, crisis by crisis. The question isn't whether Canada will have social credit scoring - it's whether Canadians will recognize it before resistance becomes impossible.

Just as historical populations rationalized their compliance until resistance became impossible, today's citizens surrender their privacy piece by piece. Each convenience accepted, each term of service agreed to, each digital ID adopted builds the infrastructure of control. The pattern repeats because it works: gradual implementation prevents coordinated resistance until the system stands complete.

The transformation of Canada extends beyond economic metrics and policy failures. Each crisis—housing, healthcare, cost of living—advances infrastructure for comprehensive social control. Digital ID requirements expand under service modernization. Financial surveillance grows through payment systems. Location tracking spreads through transportation networks.

The Bank of Canada's Central Bank Digital Currency creates programmable money—currency that can be controlled, monitored, and expired. Provincial digital identity programs establish social credit scoring capabilities. Municipal surveillance systems track movement and behaviour. Healthcare digitization enables algorithmic access to treatment.

Private corporations build commercial surveillance infrastructure. BlackRock's "smart" communities normalize continuous monitoring. Meta's platforms track social connections and influence. Google maps population movements. Amazon records consumption patterns. Each private database feeds government control systems.

The Canada Revenue Agency expands monitoring beyond tax collection. The Canadian Border Services Agency extends biometric tracking beyond immigration. Service Canada transforms from service provider to compliance monitor. Every government interaction requires surrendering more privacy to integrated surveillance networks.

Manufactured crises justify expanding control. Housing shortages normalize rental surveillance. Healthcare strain justifies patient tracking. Financial pressure forces digital payment adoption. Immigration numbers enable testing social credit mechanisms. Each solution requires accepting more monitoring.

This isn't speculation about future dystopia. These systems are being implemented now, piece by piece, crisis by crisis. The Office of the Superintendent of Financial Institutions approves social credit frameworks within banking systems. The Online Harms Act enables thought control mechanisms. Digital ID initiatives create citizen tracking infrastructure.

Today's "innovative solutions" become tomorrow's control mechanisms. Emergency measures never expire. Temporary programs become permanent. Each surveillance expansion sets precedent for the next. By the time most citizens recognize the architecture of digital authoritarianism, resistance becomes impossible.

As this analysis goes to print, Canada's political landscape shifts rapidly. Trudeau's resignation announcements and cabinet reshuffles reveal not failure of policy but success of implementation. The system's architecture stands nearly complete, ready to continue regardless of who holds office. Whether Conservative leader Pierre Poilievre's strategic silence on surveillance expansion indicates opposition or acceptance remains to be seen, but the machinery of control transcends individual politicians.

The political theatre of leadership changes masks deeper continuity: digital ID implementation proceeds, CBDC development advances, surveillance infrastructure expands. The system doesn't require specific politicians—it operates through institutional momentum, bureaucratic integration, and technological inevitability. Each crisis, each change, each transition provides cover for further implementation.

The window for awareness closes rapidly. Canada approaches a point where technological control systems achieve critical mass. Each crisis accelerates implementation. Each solution extends surveillance. The choice between freedom and control remains possible—but not for long.

This transformation doesn't arrive through revolution but through reasonable responses to manufactured crises. Each problem justifies more control. Each solution requires surrendering more freedom. By the time the system stands complete, the capacity for opposition disappears.

This examination reveals more than policy failures or economic decline. It exposes the systematic implementation of social control through crisis and consent. The evidence exists in legislation, programs, and infrastructure being built today. The choice to see it remains yours—for now.

The question isn't whether these systems will be implemented—that process advances daily. The question is whether Canadians will recognize and resist them before the window of opportunity closes permanently.

History's most chilling aspect isn't that writers predicted our surveillance society—it's that their warnings became implementation guides. Aldous Huxley's "Brave New World" didn't just foresee psychological conditioning; it provided a template for manufacturing consent through pleasure and distraction. George Orwell's "1984" didn't just imagine comprehensive surveillance; it detailed the infrastructure of control being built today.

Consider how Huxley's vision manifests in current reality. His soma drugs parallel our pharmaceutical management of dissent. His feelies mirror our digital entertainment addiction. His genetic castes reflect our algorithmic social scoring. What he presented as warning, the system adopts as methodology. The only difference? Our technology makes his dystopia look primitive.

Yevgeny Zamyatin's "We" described a world where glass apartments enabled constant observation. Today's smart homes, digital assistants, and IoT devices create surveillance more comprehensive than Zamyatin could imagine. His One State's tablets tracking citizens' movements become our smartphones monitoring every step. His numbers instead of names become our digital IDs and social credit scores.

Franz Kafka's "The Trial" revealed how bureaucratic control operates through uncertainty and procedural complexity. Today's digital systems perfect this method: automated decisions without appeal, algorithmic judgments without explanation, system requirements that constantly change. The process itself becomes the punishment, the uncertainty the control mechanism.

Ray Bradbury's "Fahrenheit 451" warned how entertainment could replace thought, how constant distraction could prevent resistance. Today's social media algorithms, content recommendation systems, and digital dopamine loops achieve this more effectively than any book burning. Why ban information when you can simply drown it in noise?

Philip K. Dick's "The Minority Report" predicted predictive policing through precognition. Today's AI systems analyze behavioural patterns to predict "social risk scores." His fictional PreCrime becomes our real predictive algorithms determining access to services based on projected behaviours.

Even seemingly fantastical works like "The Matrix" contain crucial insights: humans will accept artificial reality if it feels more comfortable than truth. Our metaverse development, digital identity systems, and virtual social spaces follow this principle: create compelling artificial environments that make surveillance feel natural.

The system's architects didn't miss these warnings—they studied them. Each dystopian prediction becomes research and development. Each fictional control mechanism transforms into technical specification. Each warning sign becomes implementation milestone.

Beyond the Mirage

Technology doesn't create control systems —it enables them. In the 1930s and 1940s, governments and institutions used IBM's punch card technology to transform human beings into data points. Each card represented a life reduced to holes in paper: ethnicity, religion, occupation, property, family connections. What began as administrative efficiency became the architecture of systematic control, enabling the identification, categorization, and ultimately the destruction of millions.

Today's systems make those punch cards look primitive. Government agencies and corporations don't just track what you own—they monitor every transaction, movement, and interaction. The Bank of Canada's CBDC development isn't about modernizing money - it's about creating programmable currency that can be controlled, monitored, and expired. Digital ID systems don't just record your basic information - they track your relationships, behaviours, and beliefs in real-time.

The pattern repeats because it works. Economic pressure forces businesses to adopt digital payments. Social coercion normalizes carrying tracking devices. Government mandates require digital identification for basic services. Each system arrives as progress, efficiency, convenience. By the time its true purpose becomes clear, the infrastructure of control stands complete.

But historical examples provide both warning and hope. Every control system has vulnerabilities. The same technology enabling surveillance can support resistance. Communities that maintain parallel structures, preserve privacy, and build independence can withstand systematic pressure.

In the Terminator films, Sarah Connor inscribes a warning that resonates today: "No fate but what we make." The choice between submission and resistance doesn't arrive in a single moment - it comes through daily decisions about participation and compliance. Each small act of maintaining privacy, preserving independence, and building community resilience contributes to the larger resistance against comprehensive control.

Yet perhaps the darkest parallel emerges from Arthur C. Clarke's "Childhood's End." In his vision, humanity faces not violent extinction but managed decline—a transformation so gradual that most never recognize it until too late. Today's population control initiatives, declining birth rates, and systematic dependency creation suggest a similar pattern. The threat isn't just to privacy or freedom —it's to human agency itself.

The mechanisms of control evolve but the patterns remain consistent. Just as the Soviet system used internal passports to restrict movement and monitor behaviour, today's digital ID systems track every interaction with government services. The East German Stasi built detailed files on citizens through human surveillance; modern systems automate this process through smartphones, smart cities, and digital payments. What once required an army of informants now happens silently, continuously, through the devices we carry and the services we use.

Yet history also shows how control systems fail. Poland's Solidarity movement created parallel institutions that bypassed official control. Czechoslovakia's underground culture maintained independence through unofficial networks. These historical examples reveal crucial lessons: resistance succeeds through community organization, parallel structures, and strategic non-participation.

Today's resistance requires adapting these principles to digital reality. When financial surveillance expands, maintain cash transactions and local exchange networks. When digital ID systems grow, preserve offline alternatives and community connections. When social credit scoring emerges, build support systems that don't depend on official approval.

The integration of control systems accelerates daily. The Bank of Canada's CBDC implementation plan reveals capabilities beyond simple digital currency: programmable restrictions, social credit integration, automated tax collection, and real-time monitoring. Provincial digital ID programs establish frameworks for comprehensive tracking. Municipal "smart city" initiatives create sophisticated surveillance networks.

But technical systems have inherent vulnerabilities. They require voluntary adoption for initial implementation. They depend on data accuracy and completeness. They need public acceptance of each expansion. Understanding these weaknesses enables effective resistance.

The population management aspects become increasingly clear. Declining birth rates, promoted as environmental consciousness, mask systematic demographic transformation. Housing costs force multiple generations into monitored "smart" communities. Healthcare strain justifies algorithmic access to treatment. Each crisis advances the architecture of control while reducing human agency.

Consider how corporate systems integrate with government control. BlackRock's "smart" communities normalize constant monitoring. Meta's platforms track social connections and influence. Google maps population movements. Amazon records consumption patterns. Each private database feeds public surveillance networks. The distinction between corporate and state control disappears.

Yet resistance remains possible through strategic action.

Historical examples show how effective resistance operates through parallel structures. Poland's Solidarity movement created independent communication networks, alternative education systems, and unofficial economic channels. These parallel structures enabled resistance to survive even under martial law.

Today's digital reality requires similar creativity.

Local Economic Networks: Build community trading systems while cash still exists. Establish local food supply chains before centralization completes. Create informal support networks while association remains free. The same strategies that preserved independence under Soviet control can bypass digital surveillance—if implemented before monitoring becomes complete.

Knowledge Preservation: Maintain physical books, offline skills, and direct knowledge transfer. The samizdat networks that preserved forbidden information in the Eastern Bloc provide templates for maintaining independent thought. Digital systems can't monitor what they can't access. Community knowledge sharing, face-to-face teaching, and physical documentation become acts of resistance.

Community Building: Develop trust networks based on personal interaction rather than digital validation. The French Resistance's cell structure shows how small, trusted groups can maintain independence even under comprehensive surveillance. Each personal connection made outside digital systems, each relationship based on human trust rather than algorithmic scoring, preserves capacity for resistance.

Technical Independence: Strategic use of technology without dependence on it. Just as underground churches maintained religious practice under state atheism, communities can maintain independence under digital control—but only through conscious effort and mutual support. Understanding system vulnerabilities enables exploiting them.

The future isn't set. Like Sarah Connor's warning about fate, our choices now determine what's possible later. The window for action narrows daily, but historical examples prove organized resistance can succeed—if begun before the systems achieve critical mass.

But Clarke's vision in "Childhood's End" serves as a darker warning. The greatest threat may not be sudden oppression but gradual transformation - a managed decline of human agency so subtle that most never recognize it until adaptation becomes impossible. The signs appear in declining birth rates, engineered dependency, and the quiet dismantling of human autonomy.

The most effective control systems don't just restrict behaviour—they reshape human consciousness. Today's digital architecture achieves what twentieth-century totalitarian regimes could only dream of: voluntary submission to comprehensive surveillance. People don't just accept monitoring; they pay for the privilege through smartphones, smart homes, and digital services.

Consider how MAID (Medical Assistance in Dying) reveals the system's ultimate implications. What began as compassionate end-of-life care has transformed into a pressure valve for systemic failure. When veterans seek support for PTSD, they're offered death as a "solution." When disabled Canadians can't afford to live, the system presents MAID as an option. The message becomes clear: those who cannot or will not integrate into the digital control architecture become unnecessary to the system.

The parallel with "Childhood's End" grows starker. Clarke's novel didn't depict violent extinction but managed transformation - humanity's quiet acquiescence to its own obsolescence. Today's declining birth rates, engineered social isolation, and systematic dependency creation suggest a similar pattern. The system doesn't need to eliminate resistance; it simply needs to ensure the next generation never thinks of resisting.

Yet historical examples prove transformation isn't inevitable. When Poland's Solidarity movement created parallel institutions, they demonstrated how alternative systems could bypass official control. When French Resistance networks maintained communication outside Nazi surveillance, they showed how human connection could defeat systematic monitoring. When underground churches in the Soviet Union preserved forbidden knowledge, they proved information could survive suppression.

Today's resistance requires similar creativity but faces greater challenges. Digital systems don't just monitor behaviour—they shape reality itself through controlled information flow, algorithmic content curation, and social credit incentives. Maintaining independent thought requires conscious effort against unconscious manipulation.

The technical systems enabling this control contain inherent vulnerabilities. They require:
- Voluntary adoption for implementation
- Data accuracy for function
- Public acceptance for expansion
- Financial system integration
- Behavioural compliance

Each vulnerability provides opportunity for strategic resistance:

- Maintain analog alternatives to digital systems
- Create local networks of trust and support
- Preserve privacy-enhancing technologies
- Build community resilience and independence
- Develop parallel economic structures

But effective resistance requires more than technical solutions. It demands maintaining human agency against systematic erosion. This means:

- Preserving face-to-face community connections
- Teaching critical thinking to the next generation
- Maintaining physical books and offline knowledge
- Creating art that questions digital dependency
- Building relationships based on trust rather than convenience

The transformation of Canada detailed in this book isn't just about surveillance or control—it's about the fundamental nature of human society. Each crisis advances not just monitoring systems but a profound reshaping of human consciousness. The question isn't just whether we'll be monitored but whether we'll remain capable of imagining life without monitoring.

Sarah Connor's warning about fate takes on new meaning in this context. The choice isn't just between submission and resistance to technical systems. It's between maintaining human agency and accepting managed decline. Between preserving the capacity for independent thought and surrendering to algorithmic determination.

The window for this choice narrows daily. Each convenience accepted, each privacy surrendered, each connection digitized makes resistance more difficult. The infrastructure of control doesn't just restrict future choices—it eliminates the ability to conceive of choosing differently.

Yet this recognition contains both warning and hope. Understanding how control systems shape consciousness enables preserving independent thought. Recognizing how digital architecture enables monitoring allows maintaining privacy. Seeing how dependency is engineered makes building independence possible.

The future isn't written. But the ability to write it differently requires action while action remains possible. The choice between human agency and managed decline happens not in dramatic moments but in daily decisions about participation, compliance, and resistance.

Like the characters in "Childhood's End," we face a transformation of human society. Unlike them, we can still recognize it happening. The question isn't whether these systems will be implemented—that process advances daily. The question is whether enough people will maintain the capacity for independent thought, community connection, and human agency to envision and create different possibilities.

The choice remains ours—for now.

Further Reading on Control Systems and Digital Transformation

- "Stand on Guard: Reassessing Threats to Canada's National Security" (2021) Stephanie Carvin University of Toronto Press ISBN: 978-1487508457
- "Digital Democracy, Digital Control" (2022) Leslie Regan Shade McGill-Queen's University Press ISBN: 978-0228014270
- "Smart Cities in Canada: Digital Dreams, Corporate Designs" (2020) Mariana Valverde and Alexandra Flynn ISBN: 978-1552669433
- "IBM and the Holocaust" (2001) Edwin Black ISBN: 978-0914153108
- "The Age of Surveillance Capitalism" (2019) Shoshana Zuboff ISBN: 978-1610395694
- "Weapons of Math Destruction" (2016) Cathy O'Neil ISBN: 978-0553418811

About the Author

Neoborn Caveman is a cultural critic and artist renowned for his incisive commentary on the follies of contemporary society. Known widely for his satirical explorations of societal absurdities on The Neoborn Caveman Show, Neoborn has established himself as a sharp-witted advocate for individual freedom. His work pierces through mainstream narratives with surgical precision, offering an unfiltered perspective on the truths often obscured by modern discourse.

With a background steeped in cultural critique, Neoborn Caveman has become an outspoken voice for those disillusioned by the conventional. His dedication to exposing hidden truths is not only evident in his public persona but is also the foundation of his latest work. This book marks a significant departure from his usual satirical tone, presenting a sobering, research-intensive analysis of Canada's evolution into a surveillance state.

Neoborn's commitment to freedom, coupled with his artistic flair, makes this work not just a warning but a call to action for those who value liberty and transparency in an age where both are increasingly at risk.